# PARTY TIME!

# PLAN A BIRTHDAY PARTY

## STEPHANIE WATSON

LERNER PUBLICATIONS COMPANY • MINNEAPOLIS

To Alex and Jacqueline. There should
have been so many more parties.

Lerner Publications Company
A division of Lerner Publishing Group, Inc.
241 First Avenue North
Minneapolis, MN 55401 USA

For reading levels and more information, look up this title at
www.lernerbooks.com.

Main text set in Gill Sans MT Std 11/14.
Typeface provided by Monotype Typography.

Library of Congress Cataloging-in-Publication Data

Watson, Stephanie, 1969–
    Plan a birthday party / by Stephanie Watson.
      pages    cm. — (Party time!)
    Includes index.
    ISBN 978–1–4677–3835–4 (lib. bdg. : alk. paper)
    ISBN 978–1–4677–4722–6 (eBook)
    1. Birthday parties—Planning—Juvenile literature. I. Title.
  GV1472.7.B5W37 2014
  793.2—dc23                                    2013041261

Manufactured in the United States of America
1 – PC – 7/15/14

# TABLE OF CONTENTS

# IT'S YOUR BIRTHDAY!

**YOU'VE BEEN WAITING FOR THIS DAY ALL YEAR.** It's the day when *you're* the center of attention. It's a time for everyone to get together to celebrate *you* and give you presents. It's your birthday!

Want to throw the ultimate birthday party? Then this book is for you. It's packed with all kinds of tips and tricks to make your big day even more special than it already is.

Feeling stumped about where to host your event? We've got the inside scoop on all the best, coolest party spots. Already decided to have the get-together at your place? Then we'll give you some tips to transform it into party central. Or maybe you're sick of the same old cake. In that case, we invite you to switch it up with our unique birthday treat ideas.

Start learning everything you need to know to plan and host your perfect birthday party. You'll soon become that person all your friends turn to when they want to know how to throw an extra-awesome party.

# CHAPTER ONE

# GETTING READY
## FOR THE PARTY

**BIRTHDAY PARTIES TAKE PLANNING.** Start thinking about your party a few weeks before your big day rolls around. Get a parent to help you organize all the details. After all, you'll need a parent's okay to throw your party anyway.

## PICK A DATE

This part seems like a no-brainer, right? You have your birthday party on your birthday. Obviously!

Well . . . not so fast. What if your birthday is on a Wednesday and you've got a big test at school the next day? What if it's in the middle of summer vacation when all your friends are at camp? Your birthday isn't always going to fall on the best day for a party. You might have to plan your party a few days before—or after—the actual day.

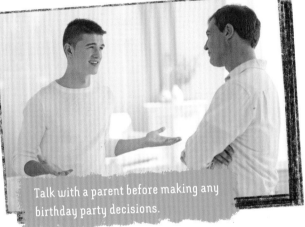

Talk with a parent before making any birthday party decisions.

Once you've picked a day you think might work, ask your friends if they're free. If most of them can come to your party, move on to the next step—which is . . .

## DECIDING WHERE TO HOST YOUR PARTY

You've got a few options here. Probably the easiest—and cheapest—is to have the party at your place. If your party's at a time of the year when the weather's nice and if you have a backyard where people can hang out, then you can host the party outside. In months when the weather isn't ideal, a basement or a big living room is a better option.

Short on space? Maybe you can borrow someone else's house for your party. Ask a grandparent or a family friend.

Here are a few other **PLACES TO HAVE YOUR PARTY** that don't cost much money:

☆ Park it! If the weather is nice, pack a picnic and invite your friends to the local park. You can play on the swings, kick around a soccer ball, and play hide-and-seek. Some parks have covered areas with picnic benches that you can rent for a small fee. You can serve your food and cake there.

☆ Play firefighter. Ask your local fire department if you can have the party at the firehouse. Your guests can ring the bell, climb on the fire truck, and maybe even slide down the poles.

☆ Explore your town. Check out your local community center or YMCA. Your friends can spend a day in the pool, climb the rock wall, or play a game of basketball in the gym.

☆ Roll on! Have your party at a roller skating rink or a bowling alley. You'll get time to skate (or bowl), plus a party area where you and your guests can chow down on pizza and cake.

Party tip: If your party is going to require special gear—jackets, shoes, or sports equipment—let your guests know if it will be provided for them.

# COOL AND UNUSUAL BIRTHDAY PARTY IDEAS

When it comes to party places and themes, use your imagination. Here are some cool ideas that will *really* impress your friends:

⇨ **Drive-in.** Turn your backyard into a drive-in theater. Ask a parent to rent a big screen or just bring the TV outside. Set up some folding chairs in the backyard. Then pop one of your favorite flicks into the DVD player.

⇨ **GO WILD.** Host your party at the local zoo. Many zoos have party packages, which include visits with the animals and your own private party room.

⇨ **Spend a night at the museum.** Some natural history museums offer sleepover parties. Start with an after-dark tour, and then curl up in your sleeping bag right next to the dinosaurs.

⇨ **STORY TIME.** Bring your favorite book to life! Love Harry Potter? Turn your house into Hogwarts Castle, complete with wizards and witches. Are you a huge Hunger Games fan? Make your party into an adventure competition with a big prize for the winner!

When signing up for a party package, be sure to find out if there is a limit to how many people you can bring BEFORE you send out invites.

8

## YOUR GUEST LIST

Now comes the tricky part. Whom should you invite to your birthday party? You might want to invite your whole class so that no one feels left out. That's a really nice idea—but hold on! First, think about how much money you want to spend. Also, consider how many kids will fit into your party place. Can you really squeeze an entire class of kids into your basement? Can your family afford to take all those people to the movies?

You also don't want to invite only fifteen out of twenty kids in your class. You'll really hurt the other five kids' feelings. Inviting ten out of twenty kids is probably okay (especially if you're sticking to the ten people you tend to spend the most time with). Just don't hand out invitations at school. You'd hate for Jen to find out you were having a party when she's not invited. *Awwwk-ward!*

To choose your party group, start with your BFFs—your inner circle. Then think about whom else from school you'd want to hang out with. Still have more room? Add a few friends you see outside of school—like kids from your basketball team or ballet class.

Party tip: If you can't invite all your friends from school, ask your guests to not talk about the party at school so uninvited people don't feel left out.

## INVITES

Once you've got a date and a guest list, it's time to send out the invites. You can do this in one of two ways:

1. Mail out paper invites.

2. Send invites through e-mail.

If you're sending paper invitations, you can buy them at the store and just fill out the details. Or make them yourself at home with some construction paper, glitter, stickers, Magic Markers, and a little imagination! For e-mail invites, websites such as Evite work well.

Once you have your invites, fill in all the details about your party. Here's a sample of everything you need to include:

What: The type of party

When: The date and time of the party

Where: The address

Special info: What do you want your guests to wear? Bring?

RSVP: This is short for *"répondez, s'il vous plait."* That's a fancy French way of saying, "Are you coming to my party or not?" Include your phone number here (or your e-mail address—or both!) so your friends can "répondez—reply."

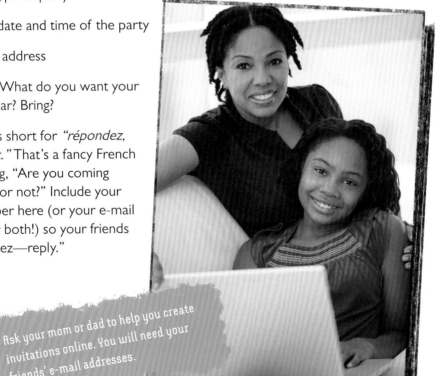

Ask your mom or dad to help you create invitations online. You will need your friends' e-mail addresses.

# PARTY

You're invited to

## Hannah's Birthday Bash!

**When:** Sunday, September 4,
from 4 p.m. to 6 p.m.

**Where:** 1234 Suburban Lane, Anytown, USA

No presents please! Instead, if you'd like to, please bring a donation for the Humane Society.

RSVP: Hannah—214-555-1212,
hannahj@anyemailservice.com

Here's an example of how your party invite might look.

## MENU PLANNING

You don't have to serve food at your birthday party. But if you're having the party around lunchtime (11 a.m.–1 p.m.) or dinnertime (5 p.m.–7 p.m.), your guests will expect to eat.

Finger foods are easiest for parties. Keep recipes simple. Include a variety of foods to keep everyone happy.

Here are a few ideas:

- ☆ Mini pizza bagels
- ☆ Rice crackers and cheese
- ☆ Pigs in a blanket
- ☆ Veggies and hummus
- ☆ Chicken-and-veggie kebobs

## ALLERGY ALERT!

Lots of kids have food allergies. Nothing will ruin a party faster than having to take one of your friends to the emergency room!

Ask all your friends before the party if they have any food allergies. If the answer is yes, be careful not to serve the foods that they can't eat. Even if your friends don't have allergies, you might want to avoid having foods that are big allergy triggers—or at least provide some alternative foods in case someone ends up needing them. Here's a list of foods that set off allergies in many people:

⇨ Milk and milk products

⇨ Peanuts and other kinds of nuts

⇨ Eggs

⇨ Seafood (for example, shrimp and scallops)

⇨ Any food with gluten (a protein found in wheat flour)

## ALTERNATIVES TO BIRTHDAY CAKE

Who said you have to eat birthday cake on your birthday? If you're over the whole blow-out-the-candles-and-cut-the-cake routine, try one of these other sweet treats:

★ Ice-cream sundaes

★ Frosted rice cereal treats

★ Decorate-your-own sugar cookies

★ Jell-O topped with whipped cream and sprinkles

★ Fruit (such as strawberries, melons, and bananas) dipped in chocolate

Party tip: Instead of a cake, make cupcakes. Frost them in different colors and arrange them on platters in tiers like a giant cake.

## DECORATIONS

You can keep the party decorations simple—or deck out your party place if you'd prefer! It's totally up to you. Theme decorations can be a fun idea. Here are some themes you might want to try:

★ *Spa decorations.* Put flower-filled vases, soft towels, plush pillows, and slippers around the room to make it cozy and relaxing.

★ MUSIC DECORATIONS. Hang some old records, CDs, and posters of your favorite singers on the walls. Hang a disco ball from the ceiling.

★ BEACH (OR POOL) DECORATIONS. Blow up beach balls and inflatable palm trees. Lay out beach chairs and towels. Put seashells and sea glass in bowls.

★ SPORTS DECORATIONS. This one's easy! Just hang your favorite sports team's banners. If you're feeling really generous, you can even hang some banners for that team your buddy loves that just beat your team in the playoffs!

Party tip: If decorating isn't your thing, ask a friend or two for ideas and see if he or she will help you decorate.

Party tip: For a more sophisticated party look with balloons, choose two colors—like silver and red—instead of multicolored.

Even if you don't have a theme, you can get creative with these party decorations:

⇨ Balloons. Tie them to chairs and tables, or fill them with helium and let them drift around the room.

⇨ Party lights. String them around the outside of your home or in your windows if your party's at night.

⇨ Streamers. Hang them from walls or in open doorways.

⇨ Cutouts of your favorite actors or musicians. Put them around the room for a star-studded event.

Ask a parent or an older sibling to help with any hard-to-hang decorations.

# YOUR TO-DO LIST

To some people, party planning can feel a little overwhelming. If that's you, don't sweat it. We've got a party-planning cheat sheet all set to go. Just follow this list, and you'll be in great shape! You can use a planner or a calendar on a phone to remind you of all the dates.

## FOUR WEEKS TO GO

❑ Decide on a date for your party.

❑ Pick out invites.

❑ Get a venue—if you're having the party somewhere other than your place, that is.

❑ Line up entertainment if you're planning to have it (whether that means hiring someone to draw caricatures or just making sure you have access to portable speakers and a phone that plays music).

❑ Write a guest list.

> venue = a place to hold a party or event. Roller rinks, community centers, and restaurants are all venues.

## THREE WEEKS TO GO

❑ Send out invites.

❑ Plan the menu.

❑ Buy or make decorations.

## TWO WEEKS TO GO

❑ Make sure your friends have RSVP'd (and if they haven't, feel free to check in with them with a friendly call or message).

❑ Get the entertainment ready—that is, pick out any specific songs you want to play or movies you want to watch.

## ONE WEEK TO GO

❑ Hang decorations.

❑ Tell your party venue how many people are coming.

❑ Buy food (with a parent's help).

❑ Fill the goody bags, if you're handing them out.

## ONE DAY TO GO

❑ Pick out your outfit.

❑ Prep the food.

❑ Run through the party schedule with a parent or a friend.

❑ Get ready to party!

# CHAPTER TWO

# THE PARTY'S ON!

**YOU'VE SPENT WEEKS PLANNING. NOW, THE BIG DAY IS FINALLY HERE!** It's time to relax and have fun with your friends. But you still have a few things left to do.

## GREET YOUR GUESTS

As the host, it's your job to greet your friends when they get to the party. When you open the door or meet friends at your party venue, start with a warm welcome. You might say, "Hi, Taylor. I'm so glad you could come to my party!"

Introduce friends who don't know one another. You could say something like, "Lori, this is Mai. She's on my swim team. Mai, Lori is in my math class."

Next, give your guests a preview of the party. Something like this will do the trick: "We're going to eat pizza in a few minutes. Then we'll play some video games and have cake."

*preview = a sample or idea of what is about to happen*

*Party tip: Don't forget that as the host, you need to get everyone talking to one another and involved in the party activities.*

19

## PARTY FLOW

The last thing you want is for your friends to be bored at your birthday party. After all, your day should be as fun and memorable as you are!

To keep the party moving, plan it out ahead of time. Here's a sample of what your party might look like:

★ 12 p.m. — guests arrive

★ 12:30 p.m. — lunchtime!

★ 1 p.m. — party games

★ 2 p.m. — karaoke

★ 3:00 p.m. — cake and ice cream

★ 3:30 p.m. — open presents

★ 4:00 p.m. — party ends

While planning can help make sure everybody has fun, do keep in mind that parties don't always go as planned. If the games are running late, just go with the flow. You don't want to switch to another activity when your friends are really enjoying themselves.

Party tip: Don't sweat your schedule if everyone is having a good time!

## PARTY ENTERTAINMENT

The right entertainment can *really* make the party. Here are some ideas that will have your guests talking about your birthday bash long after it ends:

☆ **ANIMAL SHOW.** Spiders and lizards and snakes—oh my! An animal handler from your local zoo or a farm can bring all sorts of creepy, crawly critters to your home—and teach you about them too.

☆ **Celebrity impersonator.** Can't afford to hire Austin Mahone or Demi Lovato for your party? Get the next best thing! A good impersonator looks and sounds just like your favorite singer or actor.

☆ **Temporary tattoos.** Send your guests home with a rose, a dragon, or a rainbow tattooed on their arms. The best thing about temporary tattoos is that they look like the real things, but they wear off in just a few days.

Party tip: For a different kind of temporary tattoo, try henna! You can hire someone to come and paint these intricate designs that last for weeks.

☆ **MAGICIAN.** Wow your friends with some amazing tricks. Some party magicians can hypnotize your guests or make them levitate!

levitate = to rise up into the air, as if by magic

☆ **TREASURE OR SCAVENGER HUNT.** Hide a treasure chest in your backyard or neighborhood park. Then give your guests clues to help them find the loot!

# BEST INDOOR PARTY ACTIVITIES

If your birthday party's in the middle of winter or if it rains, don't panic! There are plenty of fun games and activities you can do inside. Here are a few ideas:

→ **TRIVIA CHALLENGE.** Split your friends into teams. Have a parent ask trivia questions. Each team earns points for every answer the team gets right. The winning team earns a prize.

→ **Fashion show.** Borrow some fancy clothes from your mom or an older cousin, or pick some up at your local thrift store. Have your guests dress up and put on a runway show, complete with music! Give your most fabulous guest the "best dressed" award.

→ **DANCE PARTY.** Dim the lights, spin your favorite songs, and turn your place into the hottest club in town!

→ **PHOTO BOOTH.** Close off a corner or a closet with a curtain. Get everyone to dress up and put on funny makeup. Then squeeze a few friends at a time into the "photo booth" and get ready to take some really funny pictures!

Ask a parent to help move the furniture and any breakable accessories to create a dance room where your guests can go for it!

## PARTY PICTURES/VIDEOS

Want to remember your birthday party forever? The best way to capture every second of the fun is with photos and video.

Ask a parent to snap photos—kind of like your own personal paparazzi! With a parent's help, you can then post the pics to a photo-sharing website for your friends to download. Just don't post anything embarrassing! Your BFF might not be too happy if you share that pic where she accidentally got frosting on her nose!

paparazzi = photographers who snap pictures of celebrities and sell them to magazines, websites, and TV shows

You can also make a video of your special day. Share the video on YouTube or another video-sharing site. Just make sure you change the settings to "private" so only your friends and family can see it.

Party tip: Don't forget to get a group pic!

## OPENING GIFTS

There's no rule that says you *have* to open gifts during your birthday party. In fact, watching you go through present after present can end up boring your guests. Or your friends can get jealous—especially if you get something they really, really wanted. But if you do want to make gift-opening part of your party, make sure you follow proper etiquette.

etiquette = a code of good or polite behavior

✓ Skip the negative comments. Saying things like, "Oh, I already have this!" or "I hate this color" will only make the gift giver feel bad.

✓ Make it quick. Don't take an hour to open your gifts. Your friends have better things to do!

✓ Say thank you after you open each gift. A little bit of gratitude goes a long way.

Party tip: Before your party date, have a parent or a sibling put a variety of objects (your fav CD or T-shirt, a wooden spoon, a shoelace, etc.) in different shopping bags for you to open. As you "unwrap" each "gift," practice smiling and saying thank you in a sincere way. Bonus: find something positive to say about each item too ("This spoon will help me stir muffin batter. Thanks!").

# ALTERNATIVES TO BIRTHDAY GIFTS

Birthday gifts can be fun, but some kids feel just fine about skipping that tradition on their birthdays. If you're one of those kids, there are lots of great alternatives to getting presents on your special day. Here are just a few ideas:

» **Charity donations. Ask your friends to bring a small amount of money if they're up for it that you will then donate to your favorite charity. That might be a group that helps needy families or animals or anything you feel strongly about. Or ask for canned goods to donate to a local food bank.**

» **Book exchange. Ask your friends to each bring a book to the party. At the end of the party, have everyone swap so each person gets to bring a book home.**

» **Pictures. Have each friend bring a picture of himself or herself, taken either with or without you. Use the photos to make a memory book.**

After your party, send thank-you notes to your friends if they gave charitable donations. You can let them know the organization appreciated the donations too!

Make sure to write, "No gifts, please" or "Please bring a small donation instead of a gift if you would like to" on your invitations. That way, your guests will know that you are having a gift-free party.

# CHAPTER THREE

# AFTER THE PARTY

## EVERY GREAT PARTY MUST COME TO AN END—EVEN YOURS!

Still, saying good-bye isn't always easy, especially if everyone is having a blast.

Most parties have a set end time, which should have been written on the invite. A few minutes before the party is supposed to end, ease into your party's conclusion by giving your friends a heads-up. You can say, "It's getting close to 3. Your parents will be picking you up soon. Let's make sure you've got all your stuff, and I'll get you a goody bag."

When it comes time to say good-bye, end on an up note. Give your friends a hug. Tell them how much fun you had and how glad you are that they came to your birthday party.

## HOW LONG SHOULD YOUR PARTY BE?

In general, two hours is a good length for a birthday party. But your party might run shorter—or even much longer—depending on what you're doing. Places like roller skating rinks or movie theaters usually have set time blocks they rent out. Two hours is probably all you'll get. But if the party's at your place, you can go as long as you (and your parents) want! And if you're having a sleepover birthday party, of course, your party will go all the way to the next day.

## GOODY BAGS

You don't have to send your friends home with party favors—but if you do want to give out goody bags, here are a few ideas that don't cost much money:

⇒ *Spa bag:* Fill these bags with a nail file, mini nail polish, lip gloss, and bubble bath.

⇒ **TAKE-HOME S'MORES BAG:** Stuff this one with everything your friends need to make their own s'mores—a chocolate bar, marshmallows, and graham crackers.

⇒ Budding artist's bag: Bring out your friends' creativity with a bag filled with crayons, colored pencils, scissors, and Magic Markers.

⇒ **SPORTS FAN BAG:** Include baseball cards, a whistle, a toy car, and a basketball or football eraser.

Party tip: Check out dollar stores and discount stores for sample sizes, inexpensive trinkets, and party goods.

# HOW TO CLEAN UP THAT PARTY MESS

Parties are awesome, but cleaning up once everyone's gone home can be a chore. To make cleanup more fun, turn it into a game! First, put on some party music. Then set a timer, and see how fast you can get through each task. For example, can you take down all the decorations and put them away in ten minutes? Can you put all the leftover food and cake into the fridge in five minutes? Once your home is clean, reward yourself by playing with the presents you just got at your party or doing something else you enjoy.

Cleaning up can be a drag, but if you show your family you are willing to clean up after your party, they might let you have more parties in the future!

## THANK-YOUS

Sending thank-you notes after your party is a nice gesture—and if your guests gave you presents, it's a must. A thank-you note tells your friends you're glad they came to your party and that you appreciate any gifts you got.

You can make thank-you notes or buy them at the store. Then send them to your friends in the mail. Mailing out your thank-yous is the way to go if you got presents (including any donations to a charity). If you just want to thank everyone for coming, then a thank-you e-mail or even a text will do the trick. Attach a few pics from the party to remind your friends of how much fun you all had. You'll have them *really* looking forward to the next great party at your place!

gesture =
a way to show
that you mean
something—like
that you're
happy your
friends came
to your party

Party tip: For a fun twist on thank-you notes, buy a bunch of picture postcards—or use ones you've gotten on trips—to say thanks to your friends!

# BIRTHDAY PARTY THEME IDEAS

Birthday parties don't always have to be the same—play a few games, blow out the candles, and open gifts. Change it up by choosing a theme! Here are a few ideas to get you started:

## BACKYARD CARNIVAL THEME

Turn your backyard or local park into a carnival midway. Have a parent or other adult relative dress up like a clown. Set up a bunch of games, such as a ring toss and guess-the-number-of-candies-in-the-jar. Give out prizes at the end of the day.

## BEADAZZLE PARTY

Set up tables covered in beads, wire, and string and/or leather cording. Then let your guests release their inner artists by creating bracelets and necklaces or decorative tie-ons to use as zipper pulls or to attach to a key ring.

## BACKWARD PARTY

Ask all your guests to wear their clothing inside out—or they can put their tops, pants, and dresses or skirts on backward. Greet everyone with "good-bye!" when they arrive at your party. Then start your meal with dessert and end with finger foods. Basically, for this party, you want to do everything in an order that's opposite of what's expected.

## COSTUME PARTY

Costumes aren't just for Halloween. Ask your friends to show up as their favorite singer or superhero. Or have everyone dress in '80s clothing or in their goofiest pajamas—even if your party is during the day! Give out a prize for the best or funniest costume.

# THE PERFECT BIRTHDAY PARTY PLAYLIST

You know you want great music at your birthday bash. But maybe you're not sure exactly what tunes would be best for your party. Here are some songs that will put everybody in that Birthday Party Mood:

"Happy Birthday to You" (Your guests will sing this one!)

"Cha Cha Slide," Casper

"I Like to Move It," *Madagascar* sound track

"Fireball," Willow Smith

"Gangnam Style," Psy

"Moves Like Jagger," Maroon Five

"Hit the Lights," Selena Gomez

# FURTHER INFORMATION

**Birthdays**
http://www.parents.com/fun/birthdays
Throw the most creative party ever with the ideas on this website.

**Braun, Eric.** *Plan an Outdoor Party.* Minneapolis: Lerner
Publications, 2015.
Want to throw a cool backyard party? This book has all the tips you'll
need to get started.

**Kara's Party Ideas**
http://www.karaspartyideas.com
Party planner Kara Allen shares her secrets to hosting a party your
friends will never forget.

**Lansky, Vicki.** *Birthday Parties: Best Party Tips & Ideas.*
Deephaven, MN: Book Peddlers, 2012.
This book can help you and a parent plan your perfect birthday party!
You'll find ideas on everything from decorations to party favors.

**Lundsten, Apryl.** *A Smart Girl's Guide to Parties: How to Be a
Great Guest, Be a Happy Hostess, and Have Fun at Any Party.*
Middleton, WI: American Girl, 2010.
Whether you're throwing a party or just going to one, this book will
teach you everything you need to have a great time.

**Spoonful**
http://spoonful.com/parties
Get your birthday party planning tips in one place! Spoonful has ideas for
recipes, decorations, and party games.

# INDEX

# PHOTO ACKNOWLEDGMENTS

The images in this book are used with the permission of: © iStockphoto.com/ Nenochka (geometric pattern); © iStockphoto.com/IntergalacticDesignStudio (rolled ink frame); © Maxmilian Stock Ltd./Photolibrary/Getty Images, p. 1; © ChamilleWhite/Bigstock.com, p. 4; © JupiterImages/PhotoLibrary/Getty Images, pp. 5, 22; © Tetra Images/Getty Images, p. 6; © Cultura/Benedicte Vanderreydt/ The Image Bank/Getty Images, p. 7; © Muellek Josef/Shutterstock.com, p. 8; © iStockphoto.com/Pamela Moore, p. 9; © iStockphoto.com/LattaPictures, p. 10; © iStockphoto.com/ntstudio, p. 11 (background); © iStockphoto.com/Benz190, p. 11 (inset); © Aaron Amat/Shutterstock.com, p. 12; © Pressmaster/Bigstock.com, p. 13 (top); © Michael C. Gray/Shutterstock.com, p. 13 (bottom); © iStockphoto.com/ Sashkinw, p. 14 (top); © YanLev/Shutterstock.com, p. 14 (bottom); © iStockphoto. com/Jezperklauzen, p. 15 (top); © Tony Watson/Alamy, p. 15 (bottom); © Ulrik Tofte/The Image Bank/Getty Images, p. 17; © Dave and Les Jacobs/Blend Images/ Alamy, p. 18; © Sandeep Kelvadi's Photographs/Flickr Open/Getty Images, p. 19; © DreamPictures/Blend Images/Getty Images, p. 20; © Shannon Fagan/Taxi/Getty Images, p. 21; © Young-Wolff Photography/Alamy, p. 23; © Rob Stark/Shutterstock. com, p. 25; © Jacob Langvad/The Image Bank/Getty Images, p. 26; © Kathrin Ziegler/Digital Vision/Getty Images, p. 27; © iStockphoto.com/SandraP, p. 28 (top); © iStockphoto.com/Mamadela, p. 28 (bottom); © iStockphoto.com/Art-4-art, p. 29 (top); © iStockphoto.com/Joshblake, p. 29 (bottom).

Front cover: © Jill Giardino/Blend Images/Alamy.